MINIBEASTS UP CLOSE

Woodlice Up Close

Greg Pyers

Raintree

www.raintreepublishers.co.uk
Visit our website to find out more information about **Raintree** books.

To order:
☎ Phone 44 (0) 1865 888112
 Send a fax to 44 (0) 1865 314091
💻 Visit the Raintree Bookshop at **www.raintreepublishers.co.uk** to browse our catalogue and order online.

First published 2005 by Heinemann Library
a division of Harcourt Education Australia,
18–22 Salmon Street, Port Melbourne Victoria 3207 Australia
(a division of Reed International Books Australia Pty Ltd,
ABN 70 001 002 357).
Visit the Heinemann Library website at
www.heinemannlibrary.com.au

Published in Great Britain by Raintree,
Halley Court, Jordan Hill, Oxford OX2 8EJ,
part of Harcourt Education
Raintree is a registered trademark of Harcourt Education Ltd.

℞ A Reed Elsevier company

© Reed International Books Australia Pty Ltd 2005

09 08 07 06 05
10 9 8 7 6 5 4 3 2 1

Editorial: Anne McKenna, Carmel Heron
Design: Kerri Wilson, Stella Vassiliou
Photo research: Legend Images, Wendy Duncan
Production: Tracey Jarrett
Illustration: Rob Mancini

Typeset in Officina Sans 19/23 pt
Film separations by Digital Imaging Group (DIG), Melbourne
Printed and bound in Hong Kong and China by South China
Printing Company Ltd.

The paper used to print this book comes from sustainable resources.

National Library of Australia Cataloguing-in-Publication data:

Pyers, Greg.
    Woodlice up close.

    Includes index.
    For primary school students.
    ISBN 1 74070 235 2.

    1. Isopoda – Juvenile literature. I. Title.
    (Series: Minibeasts up close).

595.372

Acknowledgements
The publisher would like to thank the following for permission to
reproduce photographs: © Steve Hopkin/ardea.com: pp. **12–13,
19, 24**; © Dwight Kuhn: pp. **6, 22, 23, 27, 29**; © Naturepl.com/
Niall Benvie: p. **10**, /© Dan Burton: p. **7**, /© Duncan McEwan:
p. **26**; Lochman Transparencies/Dennis Sarson: pp. **8, 18**, /Jiri
Lochman: p. **14**, /Peter Marsack: pp. **4, 28**; photolibrary.com:
pp. **15, 16**, /SPL: p. **11**; © Paul Zborowski: pp. **5, 25**.

Cover photograph of a woodlouse reproduced with the
permission of Naturepl.com/Niall Benvie.

Every attempt has been made to trace and acknowledge
copyright. Where an attempt has been unsuccessful, the
publisher would be pleased to hear from the copyright owner
so any omission or error can be rectified.

Contents

Amazing woodlice! 4

Where do woodlice live? 6

Woodlouse body parts 8

Mouthparts and eating 10

Droppings and nutrients 12

Seeing and sensing 14

Legs and moving 16

Protecting themselves 18

Inside a woodlouse 20

Woodlouse eggs 22

Leaving the pouch 24

Getting bigger 26

Woodlice and us 28

Find out for yourself 30

Glossary 31

Index 32

Words that are printed in bold, **like this**, are explained in the glossary on page 31.

Amazing woodlice!

Have you ever seen woodlice? Woodlice are flat creatures that scurry in dark, damp places. You may have seen many woodlice in a compost heap, among dead leaves or under a pile of wood. Perhaps you have seen one curl up into a ball. When you look at them up close, woodlice really are amazing animals.

Woodlice are often found in large groups under logs.

There are more than 3500 kinds, or **species**, of woodlice.

Other names

Woodlice are also known as slaters, sowbugs and pillbugs. One of them on its own is called a woodlouse.

What are woodlice?

Woodlice are crustaceans. Crabs, crayfish and barnacles are also crustaceans. Crustaceans have no bones. Instead, they have a hard, tough skin, called an **exoskeleton**. Crustaceans have many legs and most kinds live in water. Unlike most crustaceans, woodlice live on land.

Where do woodlice live?

Woodlice are found in many different parts of the world. They live in the hottest deserts of Africa and in salty pools in Australia. The common sea slater lives on beaches. Most woodlice live in forests.

Habitat

A **habitat** is a place where an animal lives. Woodlice are found in a lot of different habitats. Most live in damp, dark places. The **leaf litter** on a forest floor is a good habitat for woodlice. Woodlice are also found in compost, soil, and under bark and rocks.

The cracks in brick walls can be home to many woodlice.

Woodlice that burrow

Desert woodlice dig burrows to shelter in during the hot day.

Woodlice live in these places because they find their food there. They can also stay hidden from **predators.**

Many woodlice move out into the open at night to feed. During the day, beach woodlice shelter under rocks, seaweed and driftwood. They come out to feed when the sun has set.

Living in dark, damp places keeps woodlice from drying out.

7

Woodlouse body parts

A woodlouse's body has three main parts. These are the head, the **thorax** and the **abdomen** (<u>ab</u>-da-men). The body is covered by a hard **exoskeleton**.

The head

A woodlouse's head has a mouth, two eyes and two pairs of feelers called **antennae** (an-<u>ten</u>-ay). One pair is very small and difficult to see.

The thorax

In adult woodlice, the thorax has seven parts, or **segments**. Each segment has a back plate. These look like pieces of **armour**. The woodlouse's seven pairs of legs are attached to these segments. A pair of legs is attached underneath each segment.

The abdomen

The abdomen is much shorter than the thorax. At the end of the abdomen there are two tail-like body parts called **uropods**.

antenna

head

leg

back plate

abdomen

thorax

uropod

Mouthparts and eating

Most woodlice eat rotting plants. In a compost bin, woodlice eat potato peelings, cabbage leaves, tomatoes and carrot tops. Woodlice also eat **fungi** that grow on leaves. Quite often, they eat their own droppings.

Woodlice sometimes eat the flesh of dead animals. They may eat other woodlice, even when they are alive. This may happen when a woodlouse is shedding its skin. At that time, its soft body is easy to bite.

On a forest floor, woodlice eat dead leaves and wood.

Mouth

The mouth has two jaws, called **mandibles**. These break food into small pieces for swallowing.

A bee-eating woodlouse

The sand beach woodlouse of New Zealand mainly eats the bodies of honeybees that have drowned on the seashore.

Drinking

Woodlice get water in several ways. One way is from the moist food they eat. Another is to drink it, for example, from dewdrops. A third way of getting water is by taking it in through their **uropods**.

A woodlouse's mouth is underneath its head.

mouth

11

Droppings and nutrients

Woodlice recycle their waste by eating their droppings.

Why do woodlice eat droppings?

When a woodlouse swallows food, the food moves through a long food tube to the stomach. As it moves along, the food is broken down. This releases **nutrients**, which the woodlouse needs to stay alive. The nutrients are taken into the woodlouse's blood. Some nutrients may pass out through the anus in the woodlouse's droppings. By eating the droppings, a woodlouse can obtain these nutrients.

Copper

One nutrient a woodlouse must have is copper. Copper is a metal, like iron or aluminium. The copper in the woodlouse's blood carries **oxygen**. Woodlice get copper by eating rotting leaves. When there are no rotting leaves about, a woodlouse can get copper from its droppings.

Rotting leaves supply copper for this woodlouse.

Seeing and sensing

Woodlice **sense** the world around them in several ways.

Eyes

A woodlouse has **compound eyes**. Each compound eye is made up of many very small eyes. Each small eye faces in a slightly different direction. It sees something a little bit different from the other eyes.

Some insects' compound eyes have thousands of small eyes. A woodlouse's compound eyes have just fifteen to twenty small eyes. This means that a woodlouse's eyesight is poor.

compound eye

A woodlouse does not need good eyesight because it lives in dark places.

Antennae

A woodlouse has two pairs of feelers called **antennae**. One pair is large. As the woodlouse walks, it taps these antennae on the ground in front of it. The antennae pick up smells and enable the woodlouse to find food. Smells can also lead a male woodlouse to a female.

The second antennae, called **antennules** (an-<u>ten</u>-yools), are tiny and probably have no use.

Folding antennae

When a woodlouse rolls into a ball, it neatly folds away its antennae into hollows in its head.

A woodlouse uses its large antennae to find food.

antenna

15

Legs and moving

Woodlice have fourteen legs. The legs
are arranged in seven pairs. Each pair is
attached underneath a woodlouse's body.
There is a pair of legs attached to each
of the seven **segments** of the **thorax**.

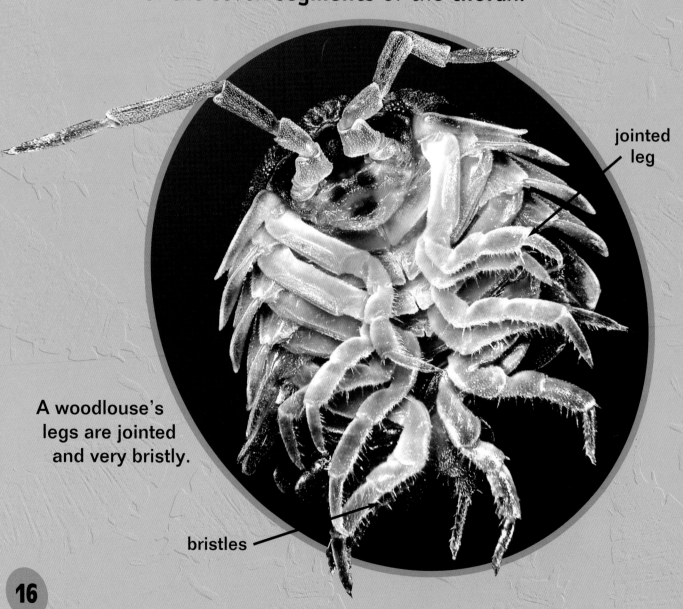

jointed
leg

A woodlouse's
legs are jointed
and very bristly.

bristles

Legs

Woodlouse legs are jointed. This means that they have separate sections joined together. All fourteen legs are the same size and shape.

Walking and running

Woodlice can move at different speeds. When they are searching for food, they move slowly. When a light comes on, or when a **predator** is about, they scurry for cover.

A woodlouse does not walk just on its feet. Half of each leg also touches the ground. The lower part of each leg has short bristles. These give the woodlouse a good grip on leaves, rocks and sticks as it walks.

Protecting themselves

Many animals eat woodlice. There is a **species** of spider that eats nothing but woodlice. Centipedes, beetles, frogs and newts eat woodlice. In Europe, hedgehogs and shrews eat woodlice.

Avoiding predators

One way that a woodlouse avoids **predators** is to hide. Some woodlice scurry away when danger threatens. Others can roll into a ball. This protects their soft undersides from attack by small predators, such as centipedes. Rolling up may also confuse a predator.

Woodlice can give off an unpleasant smell. This keeps many predators away.

A pillbug is a woodlouse that can roll into a ball. The other woodlouse pictured cannot roll into a ball.

Drying out

Many species of woodlice lose water quickly through their **exoskeletons**. Their exoskeletons are not waterproof. But this is not a problem as long as these woodlice remain in damp places.

Desert woodlice avoid losing water by staying in their burrows by day. They come out to feed after dark.

FANTASTIC
WORLD OF
WATERLIFE

FANTASTIC
WORLD OF
WATERLIFE

STEVE PARKER

Miles
Kelly
PUBLISHING

First published in 2000 by Miles Kelly Publishing Ltd
Bardfield Centre
Great Bardfield
Essex CM7 4SL

24681097531

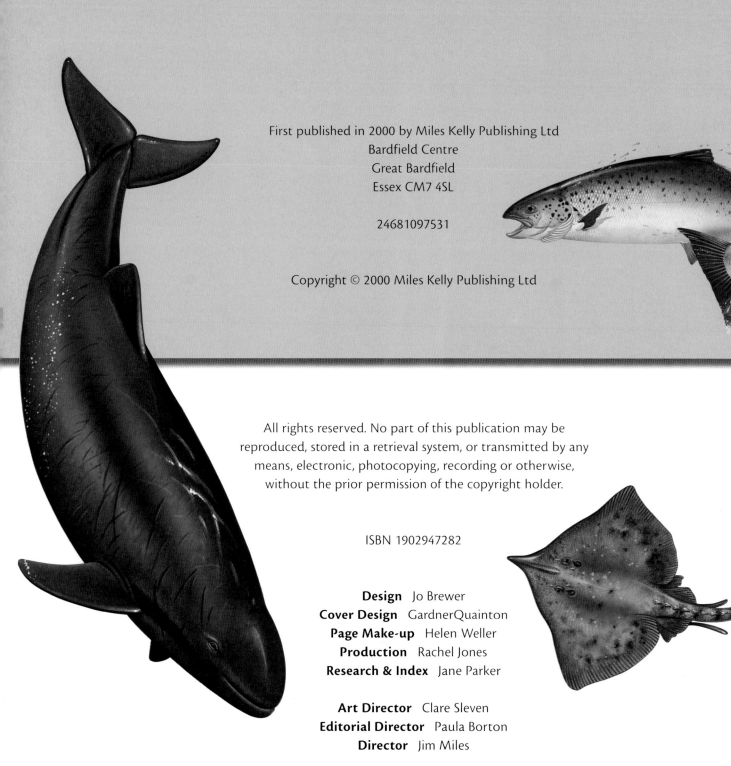

ISBN 1902947282

Design Jo Brewer
Cover Design GardnerQuainton
Page Make-up Helen Weller
Production Rachel Jones
Research & Index Jane Parker

Art Director Clare Sleven
Editorial Director Paula Borton
Director Jim Miles

The publishers wish to thank Ted Smart
for the generous loan of his illustrations.

Printed in Hong Kong

Contents

World of waterlife 6

Gills, lungs and fins – *lungfish* 8

Strange survivors from prehistory – *bowfins and gars* 10

Fish of the stagnant swamps – *bony-tongue fish* 12

A-maze-ing air-breathers – *labyrinth fish* 14

The biggest family of fish – *carp and their cousins* 16

Silvery spotted leapers – *salmon and trout* 18

Hard-shelled slow-movers – *freshwater turtles* 20

The widest, toothiest grin – *crocodiles and alligators* 22

Shy, secretive and sightless – *river (freshwater) dolphins* 24

Wings underwater – *rays and skates* 26

The most feared fish in the sea – *sharks* 28

Snakes of the sea – *eels* 30

Flying fins and needle noses – *flyingfish and garfish* 32

In the warm midwater gloom – *spiny-finned fish* 34

A tough life at the seaside – *shore and rock pool fish* 36

Dangerous or just curious? – *barracudas and mullets* 38

Fish with big appetites – *tunas and mackerels* 40

Swords, sails and speed – *swordfish and other billfish* 42

Fish in their millions – *herrings and sardines* 44

Hard-shelled swimmers – *estuarine and marine turtles* 46

Peaceful plant-eaters of the sea – *manatees and dugongs* 48

Flipper-footed fish-eaters – *sea-lions and seals* 50

Grey shapes among the waves – *porpoises* 52

Big smiles and clever tricks – *dolphins* 54

Master hunters of the ocean – *killer and pilot whales* 56

Noisy whales of northern seas – *white whales* 58

Giant hunters of the depths – *sperm whales* 60

The bottom of the sea – *deep-sea fish* 62

Index 64

World of waterlife

▶ Within the pages of this book all the animals shown in the main picture are listed in this panel. They are named in alphabetical order.

Walrus
All (or most) of the animals pictured in this book have their own entries, giving important details about their lifestyles, where they live, what they eat and how they breed.

Life began in the sea. Most of it stays there. From jellyfish to shellfish to swordfish, the oceans swarm with a vast array of creatures. This book shows water animals which are vertebrates (with backbones), mainly fish but also many reptiles like crocodiles and turtles, and mammals such as dolphins and seals.

Sea water is a 'soup' of tiny floating plants and animals called the plankton. These are food for smaller fish such as herrings and sardines. In turn the smaller fish are eaten by larger ones such as fearsome barracudas and ferocious sharks, building up the ocean food chains.

Fresh waters of rivers and lakes are also home to a huge variety of fish, from pygmy

You will always find a strange or amazing fact in this panel!

gobies to giant arapaimas in Amazon swamps. A few fish can move from salty water to fresh, by complicated tricks of body chemistry. Leaping salmons and wriggling eels attempt these perilous journeys.

Some air-breathing animals are water-dwellers. They include the biggest creatures on our planet, great whales. Others are peaceful plant-munching manatees, secretive and almost blind river dolphins, and long-tusked walruses and narwhals. All of these fascinating water creatures and many more are featured in this book.

Gills, lungs and fins

▶ African lungfish
▶ Australian lungfish
▶ South American lungfish

Lungfish look like links with the distant past, when prehistoric fish first crawled from the water, developed fins into limbs, gulped air and began to live on land as amphibians. Lungfish belong to a very ancient fish group which has been around for more than 300 million years. But they have continued to change or evolve through time and are now well adapted to life in slow muddy rivers, weedy lakes and shallow swamps. Like other fish, they can breathe oxygen dissolved in the water using their gills. But if the water lacks oxygen, for example when it is very shallow and warm, lungfish can also swallow air into their tube-like lungs.

8

African lungfish

This eel-like fish grows to 2 m long and is a fearsome hunter of smaller water creatures such as fish, frogs, crayfish, lizards and water birds. At breeding time the male wriggles and digs a hole in the sand or mud for the female to lay her eggs. He guards these while they develop and hatch.

Australian lungfish

The Australian lungfish is from a different ancient fish group to the South American and African types. It has fins with strong, fleshy bases like the famous 'living fossil' fish called the coelacanth. Also its Y-shaped, two-lobed lung is higher in the body, above the main guts, compared to the other lungfish. And it cannot survive buried in the mud if its creek or pool dries out. But like its cousins, the Australian lungfish is a powerful predator of almost any small water animal. It reaches a length of 1.5 m. These lungfish live naturally in the Mary and Burnett Rivers of north-east Australia. They have also been taken to other waterways in the region, in case accidental pollution or some other problem threatens this unique fish.

WHEN LUNGFISH GO TO SLEEP

South American and African lungfish can survive drought, when their water dries up, by burrowing into the damp mud beneath. As the dry season arrives and the rivers and pools shrink, the lungfish noses and presses the mud aside to form a vase- or tube-shaped chamber. It curls up in here and then its skin makes a layer of mucus (slime). This goes hard to form a waterproof lining or cocoon for the chamber. If the water disappears completely the lungfish seals the top of its chamber with another lump of mucus. Here it can pass the dry season, its body processes working very slowly, almost like a mammal in hibernation. This method of survival in the hot, dry season is called aestivation.

South American lungfish

Like other lungfish, the South American type does not breathe air through its nostrils as in land animals. It gulps air down its throat and gullet (oesophagus) and through a slit into its lungs. This lungfish reaches about 1.2 m in length and, like its African relative, its lower fins are long feelers.

In its cocoon in the mud, a lungfish can survive for several years. It does not eat, but gets its nutrients and energy by breaking down its own muscles.

- Bowfin
  (grindle or Great
  Lakes dog-fish)
- Longnose gar
  (long-nosed gar-
  pike or garfish)
- Spotted gar
  (spotted gar-pike
  or garfish)

The vast majority of fish belong to one enormous group, the bony fish. They have skeletons made of bone, not cartilage like sharks and rays. But among the 20,000-plus kinds of bony fish are several small groups which resemble their prehistoric cousins, almost like 'living fossils'. One is the bowfin group. It's so small that it has only one member – the bowfin. This fascinating fish lives in pools and streams in north-east and central North America. Fossils of its ancient cousins dating back to dinosaur times have been found across Europe and Asia. Gars were also once widespread. Now only seven kinds (species) survive in North and Central America.

Longnose gar
The longnose gar (shown opposite eating a threadfin shad) is a lurking predator like the other gars. It grows to about 1.7 m in length and lives in lakes and rivers throughout North America. Gars tend to wait among water plants, or alongside roots or branches, and dash out with a rush to grab their prey.

Spotted gar
The spotted gar has ideal camouflage for hiding among plants or bits of sunken wood. A gar's long mouth has many sharp teeth and the slender jaws can be flicked sideways at speed through the water to snap up victims. The anal (underside) fins and dorsal (back) fins are placed to the rear, near the tail, for bursts of speed.

Bowfin
This unique fish has many unusual features. It is named after its long back or dorsal fin which has a curve like a longbow. It also has a rounded rather than forked tail, and an almost rod-like shape with a blunt head and deep, wide body. It grows to about 100 cm in length. Bowfins are fearsome hunters of smaller fish, crayfish, freshwater shrimps, frogs and similar prey.

The male bowfin is usually slightly smaller than the female and he has a dark spot edged with yellow or orange at the base of his tail. He makes a shallow bowl-like nest on the bottom by biting away plants and swishing away mud and stones with his tail. After the female lays her eggs there he guards them fiercely. He also continues to defend the babies when they hatch.

FISH OUT OF WATER
Bowfins and gars have swim bladders which can work like lungs to breathe air, as in the lungfish (see page 8). This allows the fish to survive out of water for a day or more. Breathing air is a useful feature for fish that dwell in warm, still, stagnant water, often found in tropical marshes and swamps. This water has very little oxygen dissolved in it. So the fish obtains extra supplies by gulping air.

Another strange feature of the gars is their scales. These are diamond-shaped, thick and slab-like. They are called ganoid scales and give good protection, like armour. But they are much heavier than normal fish scales. They also limit movement because the body can bend or flex less when swimming.

The male bowfin is the most dedicated father of all fish.
He protects his young until they grow to about 10 cm long.

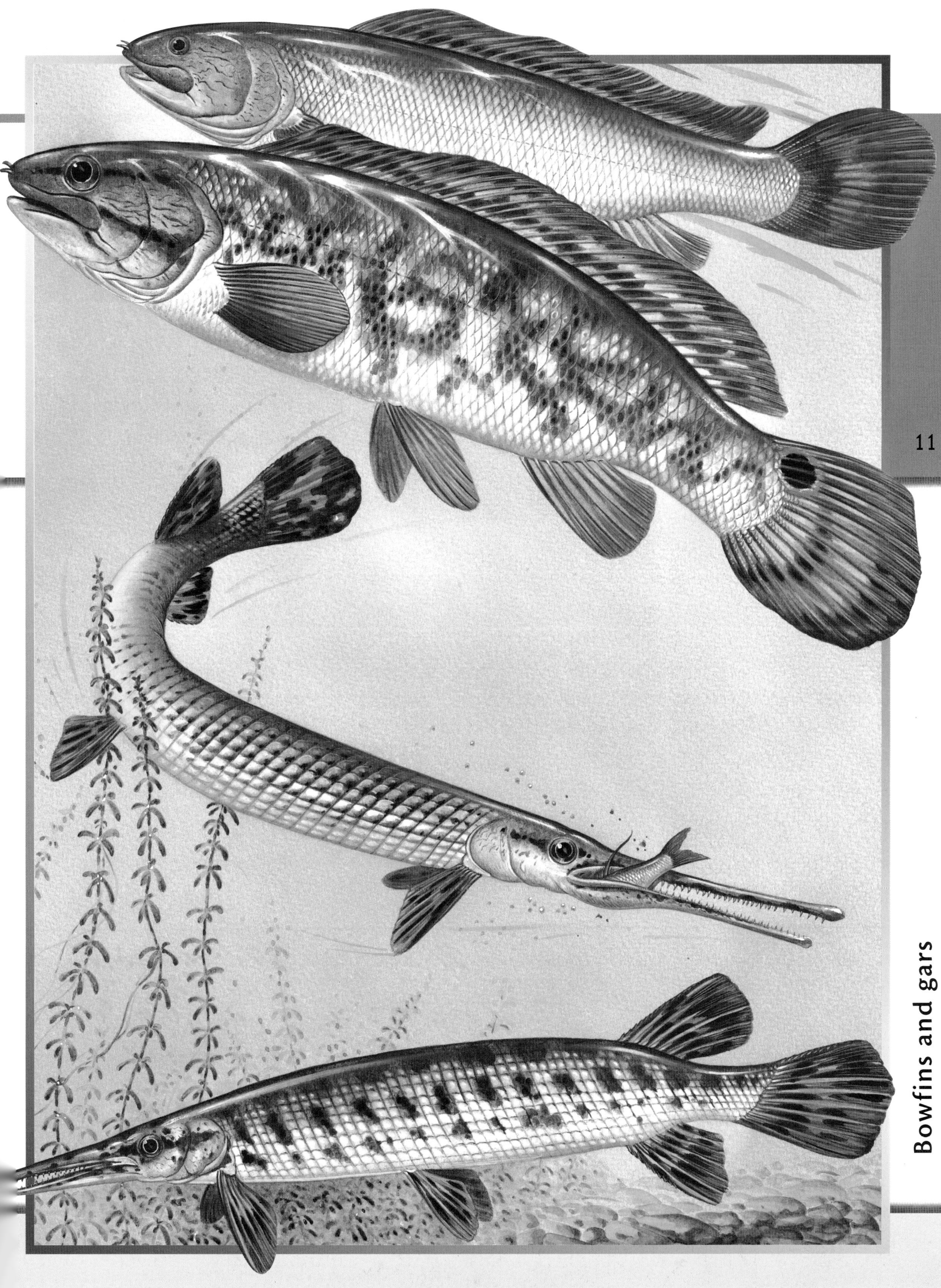

Fish of the stagnant swamps

▶ Arapaima (pirarucu)
▶ Aruana (arowana)

The bony-tongue fish are exactly as their name suggests. The tongue in the floor of the mouth is strengthened by hard, plate-like pieces of bone. When the fish bites it does not so much bring its two jaws together, as press its tongue up against the roof of its mouth. Both the tongue and mouth roof have tooth-like projections and these crush and grind the prey – mainly other fish. Bony-tongues hunt in tropical lakes, rivers and swamps. They are mostly large and powerful fish, able to burst at speed from a weedy hiding place to ambush prey. The best-known member of the group is the arapaima – one of the biggest freshwater fish in the world.

Arapaima

The arapaima is known by various local names in its swampy home of tropical South America. It can 'breathe' in the normal fish way using its gills and also by gulping air down its throat into its swim bladder. The swim bladder's blood-rich lining then works like a lung to absorb the oxygen from the air into the body. This is very useful since warm, still, stagnant swamp water is very low in oxygen.

Tales were told of arapaimas swallowing full-grown people. This is very unlikely but the arapaima is still enormous for a freshwater fish. Its vast mouth can swallow a 50-cm prey whole. At breeding time the arapaima scoops a nesting hollow in the sandy swamp bed and guards its eggs there. It also guards the babies when they hatch.

Aruana

The aruana has a very distinctive shape, its flat-topped head making a straight line with its back and almost running into its tail. The fish grows to about 100 cm long and inhabits lakes and slow-flowing rivers in warmer parts of South America. The fleshy 'tentacles' on its upturned mouth are barbels. These are very sensitive to touch. They can also feel water currents and detect or taste certain substances in the water. Like the arapaima, the aruana has a long dorsal (back) fin and a similar anal (underside) fin, both set near the rear of its body just in front of the tail. When the fish swishes its rear body powerfully these fins help the tail to thrust it forward very quickly, usually to dash at prey.

MONSTER FISH FROM THE STEAMY JUNGLE

Many tales came from the remote swamps of the Amazon region about giant fish. Some were said to be so huge that they could swallow a person, an anaconda (the world's bulkiest snake) or a caiman (South American crocodile) in one gulp – or even a whole canoe! However it is difficult to judge the length of a fish half-hidden in muddy water. Also the size of the fish probably grew each time the story was told. The arapaima can swallow large prey but it feeds mainly on smaller food including shellfish and worms. Several other freshwater fish probably grow as large, including the massive catfish of rivers such as the Mekong in Southeast Asia.

There are sightings of giant arapaimas growing to more than 5 m in length and 200 kg in weight. But 3 m and 100 kg are probably more realistic.

Bony-tongue fish

A-maze-ing air-breathers

- Climbing perch
- Fighting-fish (Siamese or Thai fighting-fish, blue and red varieties)
- Three-spot gourami

The fish called anabantoids include many types familiar from the tropical aquarium – gouramis, combtails, paradise fish, climbing perches and fighting-fish. They are also called labyrinth fish because of the way they breathe. Normally they use their gills like other fish. But often the warm, still water of their tropical swamps and pools is low in oxygen. So the fish gulps air into two special chambers, one on either side of the head behind the eye. Each chamber has flaps that form a maze or labyrinth with a blood-rich lining. The air is trapped and its oxygen passes into the blood.

14

Climbing perch
About 25 cm long, the climbing perch lives in India, Southeast and East Asia. It makes good use of its air-absorbing labyrinth organs when it crawls from the water and wriggles across land, even over tree trunks and rocks. The perch usually does this to look for new water because its pool has almost dried up. It moves on land using its strong lower front fins (pectorals) and also the spikes on its gill covers, assisted by pushing with its tail. It can travel several hundred metres, usually at night when the air is cooler and damper, and there are fewer predators.

Fighting-fish
These small fish, only 5–7 cm long, live naturally in ponds and sluggish rivers in the Thailand region. The males vary from green to brown while the females are lighter olive-brown. However they have been bred for thousands of years to produce many varieties of fighting-fish, in different colours and sizes. Some have very long fins which they spread out as a threat to the rival.

Three-spot gourami
Wild gouramis live mainly in Southeast and East Asia, some reaching about 60 cm long. But many types have been selected and bred by people to produce a wide range of aquarium fish. These include thick-lipped, kissing, dwarf, lace, honey, sparkling and croaking gouramis. They are usually peaceful but at breeding times the males may attack other fish.

WHY FIGHTING-FISH FIGHT
Fighting-fish do not fight for fun or because they dislike each other. It is a natural instinct of many male animals at breeding time to show that they are strong and fit, and so a suitable mate for the female. Also fish may contest a living area or territory, where they feed and which they also need to possess in order to attract a mate. In the wild most such 'fights' normally involve body postures and displays rather than actual physical battle. However even in the wild the male fighting-fish is quite aggressive. It lifts its gill covers, stretches out its fins and may actually attack other male rivals. People have made these instincts stronger by selecting the most agressive males for breeding.

Fighting-fish can become so aroused that they even attack their own reflections on the inside of the aquarium's mirror-like glass side.

Labyrinth fish

The biggest family of fish

- Bigmouth buffalo
- Dace (dart)
- Goldfish
- Minnow
- Nase (sneep)
- Shorthead redhorse
- Stone loach
- Pike (northern pike)

The carp family is the largest of all fish groups with some 2000 different species. They live in fresh water and are mostly strong, deep-bodied and eat small food items such as bits of plants and water-living grubs. Different kinds of carp live mainly in the northern parts of the world. They have been taken to many other regions as food fish and for anglers. The common carp is now found almost worldwide and is an especially powerful and wily fish. In addition goldfish, koi, mirror carp, golden carp, leather carp and many other varieties have been bred as ornamental fish for ponds and lakes.

16

Dace
A quick and darting fish, the dace rarely grows longer than 25 cm. It likes clean fairly fast rivers and eats flies, grubs and other small animals.

Minnow
Many small or young fish are 'minnows' but the minnow is also a distinct kind or species. It is only 10 cm long and a common victim of bigger fish.

Nase
A fish of fast and gravel-bottomed rivers, the nase lives in Europe and Western Asia. It scrapes small plants off the stones with its hard, horny lips.

Pike
The pike is not a member of the carp group – but it does eat carp. It is a powerful predator up to 100 cm long with a mouthful of sharp teeth. It dashes out of water plants to ambush its prey.

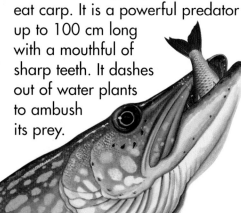

Bigmouth buffalo
This massive, deep-bodied fish reaches 100 cm in length and lives in large lakes and rivers in eastern North America. It feeds on water plants and animals such as pond snails.

Shorthead redhorse
Redhorses are types of sucker carp, named from their big, fleshy lips. They feed mainly on water insects, worms and grubs.

Goldfish
Wild goldfish live in weedy ponds and lakes across Central and Eastern Asia. They grow to 30 cm and have been bred in hundreds of colours, sizes and varieties for the aquarium.

Stone loach
This small loach, only 15 cm long, lies camouflaged on the river or lake bed by day. It grubs among the stones for small worms, shellfish and similar food.

During the spring breeding season a female bigmouth buffalo lays up to half a million eggs.

Carp and their cousins

Silvery spotted leapers

- Atlantic salmon
- Dipper (a river bird)
- Leech
- Northern grayling
- River lamprey (brook lamprey)
- Trout (sea trout)
- Steelhead trout

Leaping waterfalls and rapids, on the way up their home river to breed, salmon are among the world's best-known fish. (And the tastiest.) Along with trout, pike, charr and smelt, they make up the large salmon family with more than 500 different species. Most live in northern parts of the world and are predators, hunting smaller animals for food. Many, like salmon and sea trout, are also migratory. They grow up in a river for a few years, journey out to sea for several more years, then return to the same river to spawn (lay eggs). They probably find their way by 'smelling' the exact mixture of chemical substances in their home stream.

18

Atlantic salmon
Salmon spend from 2 to 6 years in their home river, then head out to sea where they grow up to 1.5 m long, powerful and fast as they feed on smaller fish. After between 1 and 4 years at sea they head back upriver to breed in the gravelly stream where they hatched. Most then die but some make the journey twice.

Trout
Few fish are as widespread as the trout, which has been taken to all continents for angling and as food. The variety called the brown trout stays in a lake or river all its life. The sea trout (shown opposite) is more silvery and has a life cycle like the salmon, heading out to sea and then returning to breed.

River lamprey
Lampreys are not members of the salmon family but very strange fish with an almost prehistoric body design. They lack jaws. The mouth is a round sucker edged with tiny teeth. The lamprey usually lives as a parasite. It sticks onto a larger fish, its host, and rasps its way through the skin to suck its blood and body fluids.

Northern grayling
The grayling looks like a small trout, about 45 cm long, but with a larger sail-shaped back or dorsal fin. Like most members of the salmon family it has little, sharp teeth. Grayling live in Northern Europe and Northwest Asia and feed on small water creatures such as worms and insects.

Steelhead trout
Steelheads show the typical feature of the salmon family – the small lobe-like adipose fin on the upper rear body, between the main dorsal fin and the tail. The fish's blue-grey head looks like polished metal. The steelhead trout shown opposite is about to tackle a large leech on the stony river bed.

A salmon loses up to half its body weight as it battles its way against the current to the stream where it grew up.

Salmon and trout

Hard-shelled slow-movers

- ▶ Alligator snapping turtle
- ▶ Painted terrapin (pond turtle or painted turtle)
- ▶ Spike-shelled turtle
- ▶ Spiny softshell (spiny terrapin)
- ▶ Spotted turtle

Turtles and terrapins are far from fast. But they are well protected from harm inside their hard body shells. These mainly water-dwelling creatures, along with the land-living tortoises, are members of the reptile group called chelonians. There are about 180 different kinds of turtles and terrapins living in rivers, lakes, swamps and other freshwater habitats, mostly in northern and tropical regions of the world. Many eat a mixture of plant parts, especially soft leaves and stems of water weeds, and small animals such as worms, pond snails, shellfish, baby fish and young frogs. Female turtles lay eggs on land, in sand or mud or hidden under stones and logs.

Painted terrapin
Yellow stripes along the head and neck, reddish lines on the legs and bright markings around the 14-cm-long shell identify this common North American turtle. However its patterns are very varied, especially on the bright yellow underside. It eats mainly long, trailing water plants and also water grubs.

Spotted turtle
Most turtles are not active hunters. They lie in wait for passing victims or chomp leisurely on plants. Their dull colours and mottled patterns, like the spotted turtle's dotted patches of yellow, orange or red, help to camouflage them among the shady weeds and stones at the bottom of a lake or river.

Spike-shelled turtle
Young, newly-hatched turtles have softer shells than the adults. They are at risk from many predators such as herons, fish-eagles, mink and large fish. The spikes around the edge of this turtle's shell gradually lengthen and harden over the first two years for excellent protection.

Spiny softshell
With a shell up to 45 cm long, the spiny softshell is a powerful predator of fish, crayfish, water insects and even small water birds. Its name comes from the small, spiky lumps on the front of the shell above the neck. This turtle lives in quiet ponds and creeks in eastern, central and south-eastern North America.

Alligator snapping turtle
This is the largest freshwater turtle in North America, growing to more than 75 cm long and 90 kg in weight. It lies on the bottom of a muddy lake or slow river, its ridged shell camouflaged by weedy growths to look like a jumble of stones. The turtle holds its mouth wide open to reveal a small, narrow, pale, fleshy flap on the floor of its mouth. This wriggles like a worm and attracts fish, crayfish and similar animals. If they come to check the 'bait' the turtle snaps shut its massive, sharp-edged jaws and swallows the victim whole – or slices it in half. As an alternative, the turtle can lunge upwards and grab passing prey in the sharp, hooked front parts of its jaws. The female alligator snapper lays 20–40 eggs in early summer.

Snapping turtles feed on carrion such as drowned deer and pigs, finding them by smell. They have been used to locate the bodies of people murdered and thrown into deep lakes.

Freshwater turtles

The widest, toothiest grin

- American alligator
- Black caiman (black alligator)
- Nile crocodile
- Gharial (gavial)

Crocodiles have been lurking in rivers and swamps since the time of the dinosaurs, more than 150 million years ago. The crocodilian group has 22 members including 14 species of crocs and seven types of alligators and caimans mainly from Central and South America. The final member is the curious gharial from the Indian region with its very long, slim, tooth-studded snout. It catches fish by a sideways sweep of its jaws.

Gharial
This is one of the most aquatic crocs, rarely leaving the water except to breed. It has more than 100 small, pointed teeth for grasping slippery fish prey.

Nile crocodile
The Nile croc lives in many watery areas of Africa. It grabs large animals or birds which come to drink, drags them under the surface to drown, then tears off chunks to swallow.

American alligator
Once rare in the wild, this alligator has recovered its numbers and lives across the south-east USA. The mother 'gator' builds a nest mound of old plants and lays her eggs inside. The plants rot and release heat which incubates the eggs for about nine weeks. Like many croc mothers she guards the eggs and watches over the babies for several months.

Black caiman
Caimans are similar to alligators and live mainly in South America. Largest is the black caiman of the Amazon region at 4.5 m long. It was hunted so much for its meat and leathery skin that it is now excessively rare.

The largest living reptile is the saltwater crocodile, also called the Indo-Pacific, Australian or estuarine crocodile. It grows to more than 7 m in length.

Crocodiles and alligators

Shy, secretive and sightless

- ▶ Amazon river dolphin (bouto or boutu)
- ▶ Ganges river dolphin (Ganges susu or side-swimming dolphin)
- ▶ Indus river dolphin (Indus susu)

24

Most dolphins live in the open sea. Their secretive and little-known relatives are the river dolphins from some of the largest rivers in the world. There are five kinds or species – two in the Indian region, two in South America and one in China. River dolphins have tiny eyes and are almost blind, because sight is little use in their muddy water. However they can swim fast and accurately using the squeaks and clicks of echolocation or sonar, like other dolphins (and also bats). They find their prey of fish and similar animals by sound too, grabbing the victims in their long beaks equipped with more than 100 small, sharp teeth.

Amazon river dolphin

This freshwater dolphin lives in the Amazon, Orinoco and connected large rivers in South America. Although most river dolphins are quite shy, the Amazon dolphin is inquisitive and sometimes approaches a small boat, or even comes near a swimmer if she or he keeps still and quiet. These dolphins often move around in small, close-knit groups. They are very agile and frequently swim on their sides or even upside down. Amazon river dolphins from the Amazon itself tend to be lighter pink in colour and larger, about 2.3 m long and 120 kg in weight, compared to those from the Orinoco. Another dolphin, the tucuxi, also swims in the fresh waters of the Amazon but it is greyer and much smaller, only about 1.4 m in length.

Ganges river dolphin

This is one of the largest river dolphins, reaching a length of 2.4–2.6 m. It is a powerful swimmer and often leaps straight up like a missile bursting out of the water. The alternative name of 'susu' comes from the sound these dolphins make when they breathe out through their nostrils – the blowhole on the forehead. They eat many types of fish including carp and catfish, as well and shrimps.

Indus river dolphin

The Indus dolphin is very similar to the Ganges dolphin at about 90 kg weight. It is hunted for its body oil which is used in some local medicines. Like other river dolphins, its search for food has been severely affected by dams built for hydro-electricity and to water farm crops. All river dolphins are rare and affected by overfishing, pollution, drowning in nets and traps, and noisy boats which interfere with their delicate sonar systems.

The Indus river dolphin and the whitefin river dolphin of the Chiang Jiang (Yangtze) in China are two of the world's rarest mammals. Each numbers just a few hundred.

River (freshwater) dolphins

Porpoises

Big smiles and clever tricks

▶ Bottlenose dolphin (bottle-nosed dolphin)
▶ Common dolphin (saddleback dolphin)
▶ Fraser's dolphin (short-snout dolphin)
▶ Risso's dolphin (grampus dolphin)
▶ Southern right whale dolphin
▶ Spinner dolphin
▶ Spotted dolphin

54

Some people are lucky enough to meet real dolphins swimming free in the sea. These marvellous creatures, which are smaller cousins of whales, are warm-blooded mammals like us. But they have no fur, their arms are shaped like flippers, they have no legs either, and their tails have two broad side flukes. All 32 kinds of dolphin hunt fish, squid and similar sea animals. They take in air through their nostrils, which form the blowhole on top of the head, so they must surface every minute or two to breathe. Dolphins are fast and agile in the water. They naturally leap, somersault and spin for no obvious reason. Perhaps they are having fun?

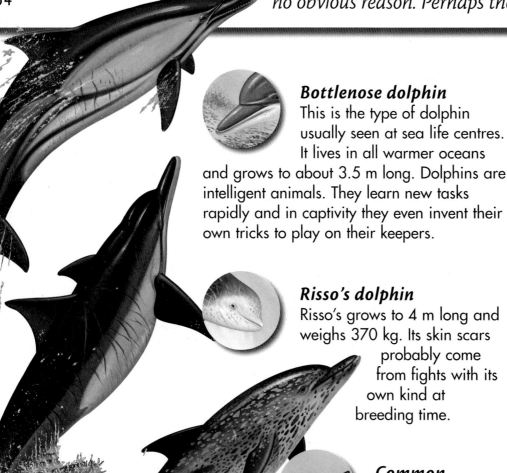

Bottlenose dolphin
This is the type of dolphin usually seen at sea life centres. It lives in all warmer oceans and grows to about 3.5 m long. Dolphins are intelligent animals. They learn new tasks rapidly and in captivity they even invent their own tricks to play on their keepers.

Risso's dolphin
Risso's grows to 4 m long and weighs 370 kg. Its skin scars probably come from fights with its own kind at breeding time.

Common dolphin
For centuries artists have painted and sculpted these dolphins, which have very variable markings and colours. They live worldwide.

Fraser's dolphin
This average-sized dolphin is about 2.3 m long and 85 kg in weight. All dolphins make clicks and squeals to find their way by echolocation and to keep in touch with their group.

Spinner dolphin
This is one of the most acrobatic dolphins. It jumps high out of the water and spins around like a top. It lives in the open ocean and eats mainly fish.

Spotted dolphin
The speckles of this dolphin may help to camouflage it in dappled surface waters. However dolphins have few enemies, mainly large fish like sharks.

The smallest dolphin is probably Heaviside's dolphin of the waters around South Africa. It is about 1.2 m long and weighs only 40 kg. The largest dolphin is the killer whale.

Dolphins

Master hunters of the ocean

- False killer whale
- Killer whale (orca)
- Pilot whale (long-finned pilot whale or pothead whale)

The killer whale is one of the world's supreme hunters. At 9 m in length and 3 tonnes in weight, it is far bigger than any land predator. It's also larger than the biggest flesh-eating shark, the great white. Killer whales are very intelligent. They live in family groups, or pods, and work together to surround prey such as shoals of fish. False killer whales are slightly smaller and do not have such a tall back fin or white patches on the sides of the body. But they too are fearsome hunters of many kinds of prey. Pilot whales grow to about 6 m long. Like the killer whales, they are not really true whales – they are very big members of the dolphin family.

Killer whale
The female killer whale is slightly smaller than the male, at about 6–7 m long. Also the fin on her back is shorter and more curved or crescent-shaped compared to the male's. His tall, pointed fin may be 2 m high – the largest back fin of any dolphin or whale. Killer whales live in all seas and oceans, even in cold Arctic and Antarctic regions. They feed on many kinds of fish, squid and similar prey. They are also the only type of dolphin or whale that regularly hunts warm-blooded victims including other dolphins, also porpoises, great whales, seals, sealions and seabirds such as penguins. Full-grown killer whales have no natural enemies and even in the wild they may survive to an age of 60 years or more. In captivity they are found to be intelligent.

False killer whale
Like the killer whale, the false killer makes a huge variety of sounds. Some are used to communicate with other members of its group. Other sounds work like sonar (sound radar) and bounce off objects. The false killer hears the echoes and so finds its way in dark or muddy water.

TOGETHER IN A POD
A typical killer whale pod has about 10 members. There is usually one large male, three or four adult females, and several youngsters who are both males and females. They may stay together for years. The babies tend to stay and grow up in the pod, generation after generation.

Long-finned pilot whale
Pilot whales are named because they often swim alongside ships and boats. They seem to guide the boat across the sea, in the way that the expert human sailor called a pilot guides ships into a port or through dangerous waters. Pilot whales tend to stay near the coast rather than head for open seas. They live in the North Atlantic and also in all southern oceans. Their main foods are fish and squid. These dolphins stay together in their pod for many years, in a group of six to ten. Sometimes several pods join together for a time to form a larger school. Like all whales and dolphins, pilot whales are mammals and breathe air. So they have to make frequent visits to the surface.

The killer whale is the fastest swimming mammal, powering along at speeds of 55 km/h.

Killer and pilot whales

Noisy whales of northern seas

▶ Beluga (belukha or white whale) (female and calf)
▶ Narwhal (tusked whale) (male)

The beluga and the narwhal make up a small group called white whales – although the narwhal is mottled cream, blue, grey or brown on its back and sides. They are both unusual among whales because they have no dorsal (back) fin, and they can bend their necks to look around and curl their lips into facial expressions. Also they live in very cold water among the icebergs and pack ice of the Arctic Ocean, especially along shores and estuaries and in shallower coastal waters. The beluga in particular is a very noisy whale. It makes a huge variety of squeaks, moos, clicks, chirrups and bell-like clangs that can even be heard above the water.

Narwhal
The narwhal has only two teeth. In the male one of these, the upper left incisor, keeps growing and becomes a long, sharp tusk with a twisted spiral pattern. It can reach nearly 3 m in length. The other tooth stays about 20 cm long. The whale's body may grow to more than 5 m long and weigh 1.5 tonnes. The female narwhal also has two teeth and one may grow into a tusk, but this is much shorter and may not even grow beyond her lips. A narwhal uses its lips and tongue for feeding, not its teeth.

Like belugas, narwhals live in small groups of adults and young. These often gather into larger herds of hundreds. The herds migrate along the coast with the seasons, to follow the shoals of fish and other food and to keep clear of the spreading winter ice.

Beluga
The beluga's many sounds and noises help it to keep in touch with other members of its group or herd. The sounds also bounce off nearby objects like rocks and animals and the beluga hears the echoes. Like a bat in air, this echolocation system helps the whale to find its way in dark or muddy water and to detect food. The beluga also 'makes faces' at other herd members by opening and twisting its mouth into a variety of smiles, frowns and grins. Belugas grow to 5–6 m in length and eat a wide range of food including fish, squid, worms, shellfish, shrimps and crabs. They feed mainly on the bottom of the sea and use their pursed lips to suck worms from the mud and shellfish out of their shells.

Beluga calf
A newborn baby beluga is 80–90 cm long. It is also brown in colour, which changes to slatey blue-grey by about one year old. Then it gradually lightens to pure white by its adult age of five years. The youngster feeds on its mother's milk for up to two years and hardly ever leaves her side during this time.

UNICORN OF THE SEA
The narwhal's long tusk looks like the head horn of the mythical horse known as the unicorn. Exactly why this whale has a tusk is not clear. Sometimes males come to the surface and use their tusks like swords to 'fence' each other. This may be to gain success in mating with females.

About one male narwhal in 50 has two tusks.
It looks like a combination of whale and walrus!

White whales

Giant hunters of the depths

- Dwarf sperm whale (Owen's dwarf sperm whale, rat-porpoise)
- Pygmy sperm whale (small, lesser or short-headed sperm whale)
- Sperm whale (cachalot, spermacet or spermaceti whale)
- Squid

Sperm whales spend much of their time in the blackness of the deep ocean, hunting their prey by the clicks and squeals of their sonar. They regularly dive more than 1000 m below the surface and stay under for an hour as they hunt near the ocean floor for fish, squid, crabs and similar food. The sperm whale's enormous head makes up one-third of its whole body length. It contains a waxy or oily substance known as spermaceti which was once used to make candles, cosmetics, creams and very high-quality lubricating oil. Sadly, hunting for this and for other body parts, like the flesh and blubber, has made sperm whales rare.

Sperm whale

The mighty sperm whale is more than 20 m long and 40 tonnes in weight, making it the largest toothed whale – and by far the largest predator or meat-eater on Earth. When whales surface to breathe they can be recognized by the pattern of moist, steamy air they snort out through their blowholes. In the sperm whale this 'blow' is angled forwards and to the left.

The massive bulging head of this whale is filled mainly by the spermaceti organ, which has layers of oily wax. These act as a kind of sound-lens to focus the whale's huge grunts of low-power sound which can stun its prey. The spermaceti organ also works as a buoyancy device. As the whale descends it becomes denser or heavier, making the whale less buoyant and so the dive is easier.

Dwarf sperm whale

Similar in shape to a porpoise, without the usual sperm whale's bulging forehead, the dwarf sperm whale reaches about 2.5 m in length. It is found most often in warmer seas, especially off the coasts of South Africa, India and Australia, and rarely in the open ocean like the pygmy sperm whale.

Pygmy sperm whale

Pygmy sperm whales grow to about 3.4 m long and 500 kg (half a tonne) in weight. They have a varied diet including shrimps, crabs, fish, octopus and cuttlefish as well as plenty of the usual squid. They catch their food at depths of about 100 m, in coastal waters and far out at sea.

BATTLE OF THE TITANS

Sperm whales sometimes plunge down 2000 m or more for two hours or longer. After returning to the surface for a couple of minutes to breathe they descend again into the depths. Sometimes a group of sperm whales dive together and work as a team to round up their prey. Like dolphins, they find food by sonar or echolocation, making squeaks, clicks and grunts that bounce off nearby objects. A sperm whale has up to 50 cone-shaped teeth in its slender lower jaw but no teeth showing in the upper jaw. Its skin is scarred by marks from the suckers and the hard, horny, beak-like mouth of its deadly enemy. This is also its biggest prey, with a 6-m body and 10-m tentacles – the giant squid.

Ambergris was once used to make the delicate scents of very expensive perfumes. Which is odd because this substance comes from inside the guts of sperm whales!

Sperm whales

The bottom of the sea

▶ Dragonfish
▶ Gulper eel
  (swallower eel)
▶ Long-rod
  anglerfish
▶ Sloane's viperfish
▶ Snaggletooth
▶ Tassel-chinned
  anglerfish
▶ Tripod fish

The world's biggest habitat is also its most mysterious. The ocean depths are endlessly black and cold. Fish and other animals live on the 'rain' of rotting debris floating down from above – or eat each other.

62

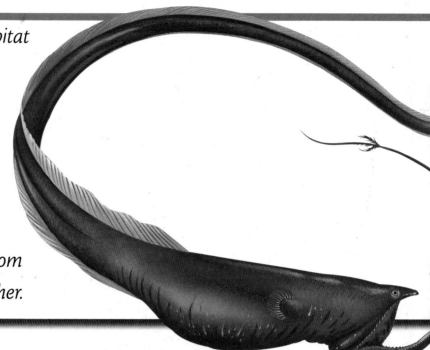

Gulper eel
Prey is scarce in the vast blackness of the deep ocean, so fish like the gulper have large mouths to grab whatever they can. This eel is a relative giant of the depths at 60 cm long.

Tripod fish
The tripod fish 'walks' along the soft mud of the sea bed on the long spines of its two lower side fins (pelvics) and lower tail. It probably eats small shrimps and similar shellfish.

Sloane's viperfish
The first spine or ray on the back (dorsal) fin of the viperfish is very long and flexible. It has a blob-like tip that glows in the darkness. Small creatures come to investigate and the viperfish grabs them in its wide, gaping jaws lined with long, needle-shaped teeth. The viperfish looks fearsome and is one of the larger predators of the ocean depths. Yet it is only 30 cm long. The general lack of food in the deep sea means animals are mostly small.

Snaggletooth
Several deep-sea fish have rows of glowing or bioluminescent spots along their sides. These may signal to others of their kind at mating time.

Long-rod anglerfish
The body of this anglerfish is only 15 cm long but its bendy, whip-like 'fishing rod' can be more than 20 cm in length.

Tassel-chinned anglerfish
Hardly larger than your thumb, this anglerfish has extraordinary fleshy tassels on its chin that resemble seaweed.

Dragonfish
Like snaggletooths, dragonfish are predators of smaller creatures. They rise nearer the surface at night to follow their prey such as very young squid.

The tripod fish is one of the deepest dwelling of all fish, found more than 6000 m below the surface.

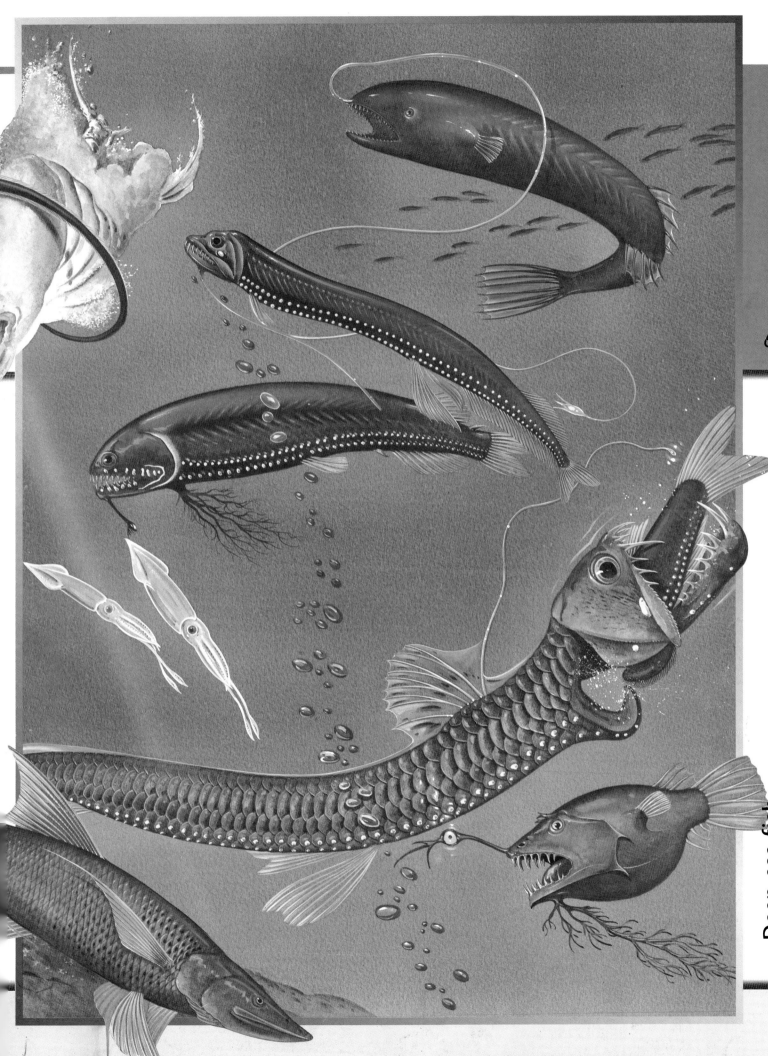

Deep-sea fish

Index

A

African lungfish 8–9
Alewife 44–45
alligator,
    American 22–23
    Black 22–23
Alligator snapping turtle 20–21
Amazon manatee 48
Amazon river dolphin 24
American alligator 22–23
American manatee 48–49
anabantoids 14–15
anchovies 38
anglerfish,
    Long-rod 62–63
    Tassel-chinned 62–63
Arapaima 12–13
Aruana (Arowana) 12–13
Atlantic flyingfish 32–33
Atlantic gizzard shad 44–45
Atlantic guitarfish 26–27
Atlantic herring 44–45
Atlantic mackerel 40–41
Atlantic manta 26–27
Atlantic menhaden 44–45
Atlantic salmon 18–19
Australian crocodile 22
Australian lungfish 8–9

B

Ballyhoo 32–33
Barbu 38–39
barracuda,
    Great 38–39
    Southern 38–39
Basking shark 28–29
Becuna 38–39
Beluga (Belukha) 58–59
beryciform fish 34
Bigmouth buffalo 16–17
billfish 42
Black alligator 22–23
Black caiman 22–23
Blue bobo 38–39
Blue marlin 42–43
Blue shark 28–29
Blue stingray 26–27
Bluefin tuna (tunny) 40–41
Blue-spotted stingray 26–27
bobo, Blue 38–39
bony fish 10
bony-tongue fish 12–13
Bottlenose (bottle-nosed) dolphin 54–55
Bouto (boutu) 24
Bowfin 10–11
Brook lamprey 18–19
Brown trout 18
buffalo, Bigmouth 16–17
Burmeister's porpoise 52–53

C

Cachalot whale 60–61
caiman, Black 22–23
Caribbean manatee 48–49
carp,
    Golden 16
    Leather 16
    Mirror 16
    Sucker 16
catfish 12
Cavalla 40–41
Char 18
chelonians 20
Climbing perch 14–15
Coelocanth 8
combtail fish 14
Common dolphin 54
Common dragonet 36–37
Common eel 30–31
Common mackerel 40–41
Common porpoise 52–53
Common skate 26–27
Conger (eel) 30–31
Croaking gourami 14–15
crocodile,

Australian 22
Estuarine 22
Indo–Pacific 22
Nile 22–23
Saltwater 22

D

Dace 16–17
Dart 16–17
Dealfish 34–35
Devil fish 26–27
Dipper 18–19
dogfish 28,
    Great Lakes 10–11
dolphin,
    Amazon river 24
    Bottlenose (bottle-nosed) 54–55
    Common 54
    Fraser's 54–55
    Ganges river 24–25
    Grampus 54–55
    Heaviside's 54
    Indus river 24–25
    Risso's 54–55
    Saddleback 54
    Short-snout 54–55
    Side-swimming 24–25
    Southern right whale 54–55
    Spinner 54
    Spotted 54
    Whitefin river 24
dolphins 24, 54, 56
Dragonet 36–37
    Common 36–37
    Spotted 36–37
Dragonfish 62–63
Dugong 48–49
Dwarf sperm whale 60–61
Dwarf gourami 14–15

E

eel,
    Common 30–31
    Conger 30–31
    European 30–31
    Green moray 30–31
    Gulper 62–63
    Pink snake 30–31
    Swallower 62–63
Estuarine crocodile 22
European eel 30–31
European mackerel 40–41
European skate 26–27

F

False killer whale 56–57
Fighting-fish (Siamese or Thai) 14–15
flatfish 26
Flyingfish 32–33
    Atlantic 32–33
    Four-finned 32–33
    Two-finned 32–33
Four-finned flyingfish 32–33
Fraser's dolphin 54–55

G

Ganges river dolphin 24–25
Ganges susu 24–25
gar (gar-pike or garfish),
    Longnose 10–11
    Spotted 10–11
Garfish 32–33
Gavial (Gharial) 22
Giant squid 60
Gizzard shad 44–45
goby,
    Neon 36–37
    Pallid 36–37
    Philippines dwarf 36
    Tiger 36–37
Golden carp 16
Goldfish 16–17
gourami,

Croaking 14
Dwarf 14
Honey 14
Kissing 14
Lace 14
Sparkling 14
Thick-lipped 14
Three-spot 14–15
Grampus dolphin 54–55
grayling, Northern 18–19
Great barracuda 38–39
Great Lakes dogfish 10–11
Great white shark 28–29
Greater sand-eel 36–37
Green moray (eel) 30–31
Green turtle 46–47
Grindle 10–11
Gulper eel 62–63

H

halfbeaks 32
Harbour porpoise 52–53
Hawksbill turtle 46–47
Heaviside's dolphin 54
herring,
    Atlantic 44–45
    Wolf 44
Honey gourami 14–15
Houndfish 32–33
hound-shark, Starry 28–29

I

Indian Ocean sea cow 48–49
Indo-Pacific crocodile 22
Indus river dolphin 24–25
Indus susu 24–25

J

John Dory 34–35

K

Killer whale 54, 56–57
killifish 32
King mackerel 40–41
Kingfish 40–41
Kissing gourami 14–15
Koi 16

L

labyrinth fish 14–15
Lace gourami 14–15
lamprey,
    Brook 18–19
    River 18–19
lamprey, River (Brook) 18–19
lampridiform fish 34
lance, Sand 36–37
Lantern-eye 34–35
Leather carp 16
Leatherback 46–47
Leopard seal 50–51
Lesser sperm whale 60–61
Loggerhead 46–47
Longnose gar (gar-pike, garfish) 10–11
Long-finned pilot whale 56–57
Long-jawed squirrelfish 34–35
Long-rod anglerfish 62–63
lungfish 10,
    African 8–9
    Australian 8–9
    South American 8–9

M

mackerel,
    Atlantic 40–41
    Common 40–41
    European 40–41
    King 40–41
    Spanish 40–41
Mako shark 28
manatee,

Amazon 48
American 48–49
Caribbean 48–49
Senegal 48
South American 48
West African 48
West Indian 48–49
Maneater shark 28–29
Manta ray 26–27
marine turtles 46–47
marlin,
    Blue 42–43
    White 42–43
marlins 40
menhaden, Atlantic 44–45
Minnow 16–17
Mirror carp 16
Mossbunker 44–45
mullet, Striped 38–39

N

Narwhal 58–59
Nase 16–17
needlefish 32
Neon goby 36–37
Nile crocodile 22–23
Northern elephant seal 50
Northern grayling 18–19
Northern pike 16

O

Oarfish 34–35
Opah 34–35
Orca 56–57
Owen's dwarf sperm whale 60–61

P

Pacific sardine 44–45
Painted terrapin (turtle) 20–21
Pallid goby 36–37
Paradise fish 14
perch, Climbing 14–15
perch-like fish 36, 38, 40, 42
Philippines dwarf goby 36
Picuda 38–39
Pike 16, 18,
    Northern 16
Pilot whale 56–57
Pink snake eel 30–31
pinnipeds 50
Pirarucu 12–13
Pond turtle 20–21
porpoise,
    Burmeister's 52–53
    Common 52–53
    Harbour 52–53
    Rat 60–61
    Spectacled 52
Pothead whale 56–57
Pygmy sperm whale 60–61

R

Rat porpoise 60–61
redhorse, Shorthead 16–17
Risso's dolphin 54–55
River lamprey 18–19

S

Saddleback dolphin 54
Sailfish 42–43
salmon, Atlantic 18–19
Saltwater crocodile 22
Sand lance 36–37
Sandbar shark 28–29
sand-eel, Greater 36–37
sardine, Pacific 44–45
Sawfish 26
Sea trout 18–19
Sea cow 48–49
    Indian Ocean 48–49
Sea pig 48–49
seal,
    Leopard 50–51
    Northern elephant 50

sea-lion, Steller 50–51
Senegal manatee 48
sennet, Southern 38–39
shad,
    Atlantic 44–45
    Gizzard 44–45
    Threadfin 10
shark,
    Basking 28–29
    Blue 28–29
    Great white 28–29
    Mako 28
    Maneater 28–29
    Sandbar 28–29
    Tiger 28
    Whale 28–29
    White death 28–29
    White pointer 28–29
sharks 34
Short-headed sperm whale 60–61
Short-snout dolphin 54–55
Shorthead redhorse 16–17
Siamese fighting fish 14–15
Side-swimming dolphin 24–25
silversides 32
sirenians 48–49
Skipjack tuna 40–41
Sloane's viperfish 62–63
Small sperm whale 60–61
Smelt 18
smooth-hound, Starry 28–29
Snaggletooth 62–63
Sneep 16–17
South American lungfish 8–9
South American manatee 48
Southern barracuda 38–39
Southern right whale dolphin 54–55
Southern sennet 38–39
Spanish mackerel 40–41
Sparkling gourami 14–15
Spectacled porpoise 52
Sperm whale 60–61
Spermacet (Spermaceti) whale 60–61
Spike-shelled turtle 20–21
Spinner dolphin 54
Spiny softshell 20–21
Spiny terrapin 20–21
spiny-finned fish 36, 38, 40, 42
Spotted dolphin 54
Spotted dragonet 36–37
Spotted eagle ray 26–27
Spotted gar (gar-pike, garfish) 10–11
Spotted turtle 20–21
squid, Giant 60
squirrelfish, Long-jawed 34–35
Starry hound-shark 28–29
Starry smooth-hound 28–29
Steelhead trout 18–19
Steller sea-lion 50–51
Stone loach 16–17
Striped mullet 38–39
Sucker carp 16
susu,
    Ganges 24–25
    Indus 24–25
Swallower eel 62–63
Swordfish 40, 42–43

T

Tassel-chinned anglerfish 62–63
tasselfins 38
Thai fighting fish 14–15
Thick-lipped gourami 14–15
Threadfin shad 10
threadfins 38
Three-spot gourami 14–15
Tiger goby 36–37
Tiger shark 28

toothcarps 32
tortoises 20
Tripod fish 62–63
Trout 18–19,
    Brown 18
    Sea 18–19
    Steelhead 18–19
Tucuxi 24
tuna (tunny),
    Bluefin 40–41
    Skipjack 40–41
turtle,
    Green 46–47
    Leatherback 46–47
    Loggerhead 46–47
turtles, marine 46–47
Tusked whale 58–59
Two-finned flyingfish 32–3

V

viperfish, Sloane's 62–63

W

Wahoo 42–43
Walrus 50–51
West African manatee 48
West Indian manatee 48–49
whale,
    Cachalot 60–61
    Dwarf sperm 60–61
    False killer 56–57
    Killer 54, 56–57
    Lesser sperm 60–61
    Long-finned pilot 56–57
    Owen's dwarf sperm 60–61
    Pilot 56–57
    Pothead 56–57
    Pygmy sperm 60–61
    Short-headed sperm 60–61
    Small sperm 60–61
    Sperm 60–61
    Spermacet (Spermaceti) 60–61
    Tusked 58–59
    White 58–59
Whale shark 28–29
White death shark 28–29
White marlin 42–43
White pointer shark 28–2
White whale 58–59
Whitefin river dolphin 24
Wolf herring 44

Z

zeiform fish 34